Endure
Lessons from finishing an Ironman Triathlon

Adam Lofquist

Copyright © 2016 Adam Lofquist

All rights reserved.

ISBN-10: 1539620972
ISBN-13: 978-1539620976

DEDICATION

To Katie and Aaron for the journey of a lifetime that changed my life.

I would also like to acknowledge a number of people that helped me get this book to where it is. Thank you to my coach, Brian Drury, who helped me get this off the ground, to Erika Block for all of your great advice on writing a book, and to Sarah Beckman for editing. Sam Benjamin, Brian Gruender, and Josh Pierce, thank you for the early morning runs and the laughter and love. Christian and Tiffany Jensen, thank you for starting an amazing organization that made this all possible. Marissa Hunnel, thank you for giving up your time with your husband to allow him to be a part of this. Kris Eul, Josh Fonza, and Matt Jadin, thank you for spending some miles with me and making the journey so much more enjoyable. Thank you to the entire support crew that gave up there weekend to help make Team Katie successful. Thank you Chris and Matt Neuman, for trusting us with your daughter. Don and Gayle Boldt, thank you for always treating me like your family and for always cheering me on. To my Grandparents, thank you for all of your support. There are so many other people that I would like to thank, I hope you know who you are. Thank you for helping me get to this point. Thank you to my friends, for putting up with my crazy ideas and supporting me in the journey. Thank you to my family, especially my parents, who have always supported my crazy ideas. I am so lucky to have you in my life.

CONTENTS

THE START   01

MINDSET   04

DEDICATION   08

LOVE   11

TEAMWORK   15

EMBRACE THE SUCK   18

THE START

We often hear stories about people who have gone through terrible tragedies. They have lost loved ones, overcome addictions, and had their own demons to face. These people are incredible, and their stories are inspiring, but at times they can be overwhelming.

It was overwhelming to me because my story never seemed to be enough, or to be honest, I never seemed like enough. I told myself that I could never come close to being as strong or as great as those people that have had to face such hard challenges.

I have a family that loves and supports me. There have been no great tragedies in my life that shook the foundation of who I am. While I am incredibly thankful for this, I allowed it to give me the wrong mindset in life. I allowed myself to just get by with enough, and to let things happen to me instead of making them happen.

Despite the best efforts of my parents, I was headed towards an average life, and I was completely okay with it. I was okay with it, not because I wanted to settle, but because I did not know that there was a world of opportunity out there for me, one full of challenges that would change my life.

This book is dedicated to people like me. If you think you are average, you are not, you are so much more. We may not have been given the challenges that others have, but that does not mean we cannot seek them out. Life is about seeking out the challenges that will help you grow. Choosing the challenge will hurt, but it is worth it. All of the challenges I have faced on and off the course have made me a better person. My hope is that with this book, I will convince you to take your next step into a challenge that will change your life.

The climax of it all is Ironman Wisconsin 2014, where Aaron Hunnel, Katie Neuman and myself were in Lake Mendota waiting for the race to begin. Aaron and I would be pushing and pulling Katie through the entire 140.6 miles. Katie has Cerebral Palsy, and without us she would never be able to start. But without her, we would never have been able to finish.

The greatest part, the finish line of Ironman, was just the starting line to a life I could never have imagined. Here is to finishing, but to never being finished.

Notes: THE START

MINDSET

I am often asked how I can do (or why I would want to do) an Ironman, a 100 mile run, or even a marathon. It all comes down to mindset.

I remember the day that my Ironman journey began. I drove down to Madison, Wisconsin the Saturday before Ironman for two specific reasons.

The first was to see one of my best friends, Christian Jensen, compete in his first Ironman with our friend, Mary Cox. Christian and Mary did the same thing Aaron and I did with Katie, but solo.

The second reason was to volunteer at the race, so I could sign up for next year's race. Ironman Wisconsin has a policy where if you volunteer for the event you can sign up the day after the race for next year's race.
I had never experienced an Ironman until that Sunday, but I had this voice inside of me that told me to just go do it, sign up for it, and see what happens.

I woke up at 5:30 a.m. on Sunday and made my way to the start area. My volunteer shift was later in the day, so I was able to see Christian and Mary start the race.

I volunteered to work the first part of the bike to run transition. This meant handing athletes their gear bags as they came into the transition area. I am really glad that I chose that task, because it gave me a good idea of the flow.

I remember Christian and Mary crossing the finish line. It was incredible.

At 5:30 a.m. the next day, I made my way the registration line. I thought by going that early it would be plenty of time to get near the front. I was wrong. There was already a line of people waiting to sign up. I sat down behind the person in front of me, in disbelief that I was actually about to sign up for the Ironman.

When the doors opened, we all started to filter into where we would register for Ironman 2014. I filled out my paperwork, handed over my credit card, and it was done. I still remember my bib number: 537.

When I decided to sign up and when I was signing up, I was not inspired by anything in particular. It was just something that I wanted to do, so I went out and did it.

I am told what I do is inspiring, and I appreciate hearing it. However, at times, inspiration is not enough.

Inspiration is not the key to success, your mindset is. Your inspiration is impacted by the world around you. Your inspiration is affected by what you see, hear, and experience. There is no problem with this unless it is all we rely on.

Mindset is king. Mindset is the most powerful tool we have. The greatest part is that you or anyone can have the mindset of a champion. You can have the mindset to take on the world and to be the best version of yourself.

It is incredibly powerful to take control of your mindset and take on the world. It is freeing to know that you, and you alone, are in charge of your success and that you can do whatever you want. How freaking powerful is that?

I do not want to just inspire people. I want to help people change their mindset about what they can accomplish in their life. That does not take inspiration. It takes a new way of thinking.

Lessons:

Mindset will trump inspiration every time.

Inspiration can hinder success.

Anyone can have the mindset of a champion.

Apply:

Write down a goal that you want to accomplish. Ask yourself why you want to do it. Continue to ask why for each answer you give. The objective is to get to the driving force behind your goal or your mindset.

Here is an example:

Complete an Ironman.

Why: It was something that I felt called to do. I wanted the challenge of a big event.

Why: I was tired of the current distances I had completed. I wanted more.

Why: I wanted to see how far I could go, and how much I could do.

Why: I do not want to settle on anything in my life.

Mindset: The only way I am going to accomplish what I want is by pushing myself outside my comfort zone to become unstoppable.

Notes: MINDSET

DEDICATION

Ironman is more than race day; it is about the journey. I know it sounds cliché, but until you actually experience what it takes to just get to the start line, you will never know how true it is.

There is no specific moment in my journey that I remember about dedication but rather a few key concepts.

Dedication is getting up and getting that workout in. Every day my alarm went off, and I had the choice to get up early and get my workout in or to just skip it. I was tired, but I got up anyway and did the workout. There were days where I was sore from a workout the day before, but I still had more to do so I went out there and I did it.

Dedication is giving up what you currently have to get what you want. I gave up a lot just to get to the start line. Everyone does. I gave up time with my family and friends, sleep, and having a full social life. I gave up the life I had to get the life that I wanted.

During the "hell weeks" of training, as they are so lovingly called, I worked 40 hours a week and trained for another 30 hours. During these weeks I had my highest mileage and was only at my apartment to eat or sleep.

To accomplish something extraordinary takes an extraordinary amount of dedication. It takes giving up what you currently do to get where you want to go. This is true for more than Ironman. Getting what you want in life requires dedication.

Lessons:

Dedication to your goal is a key to success.

We will face distractions that try to take us away from our dedication and our goal. We need to focus on the reason that we started.

Take moments to enjoy the journey of accomplishing what you want to do in your life.

Dedication to your cause or goal helps you push past the pain. Stop when you are done not tired.

In the end, it was not one workout that made a difference but the accumulation of workouts. Success is the same way. It is not one big moment but rather many small moments.

Apply:

Pick a goal that you have and write it down on the top of a piece of paper. Below that write down one daily action item to help you reach that goal and when in your day you will make it happen. Do not over think it. For me to write this book I dedicated 20 minutes of writing a day to help me get there. The great thing is that the first draft took only a week.

Adam Lofquist

Notes: DEDICATION

LOVE

I remember my first triathlon. It was a sprint triathlon. The part that I remember the most about it was the swim. It was a horrible experience.

As I got closer and closer to the water, panic crept closer and closer to me. I doubted if could do this. As I entered the water, I tried to calm my nerves. I started walking out to where we could start to swim and I tried to dive in but I could not. I just kept walking and walking until I could not touch the bottom anymore.

I tried to start swimming, but I could not control my panic attack. I spent the quarter mile swim with my head out of the water doggy paddling. I hated it.

Swimming sucks. Swimming in a pool is even worse. You just go back and forth, lap after lap and at times you lose track of your laps so you spend the rest of your swim wondering what lap you are really on.

I hate the drills that never seemed to pay off for me.

I hate getting in and out of the water. You jump in and you are cold. You get out and you are cold. Then you jump back in again and are cold again.

The pool is a boring place where your mind wanders, and all I could think about was how much swimming sucked. How much I wished I could be doing anything else besides swimming.

What does my hate for swimming have to do with love? It has everything to do with love. Love and hate are not at opposite sides of the spectrum. They are tied together closely. Everything that you love has some part of it that you hate.

We are told to "do what you love" and I agree, people should do what they love, but this advice is taken out of context. What it should really be is "Do something that you love so much it will get you to do what you hate."

As strange as it may sound, I love Ironman. I love every aspect of the day. I love the challenge of pushing myself further and seeing what I am made of. I love the athletes, spectators, and volunteers. I love the finish line and I love seeing other people achieve their dreams by crossing that line.

If I only did what I loved, I never would have completed a triathlon, let alone an Ironman. I did what I loved so much (pushing my body to new limits) that I was okay doing what I hated (swimming).

Lessons:

If we just do what we love we get nowhere. Focus on doing what we love so much that we will do what we hate.

Pain is part of love, it is part of growth, stop running away from it.

Apply:

Think of one thing that you have always wanted to do. Take a sheet of paper and on top write it down. Draw a line down the middle. On the left side write "Love," and on the right side write "Hate." Write down all of the things that you love about your goal, and then write down all the things that you will hate about it.

As an example if your goal was to take a trip to Hawaii on the "Love" side you could write: scenery, culture, surfing, whale watching or weather. On the "Hate" side you could write: saving money, not going out, less vacation time or travel. This way you can gain a clear understanding of the cost and benefits to doing what you love.

If at the end the hate outweighs the love, do not do it.

Adam Lofquist

Notes: LOVE

TEAMWORK

Crossing the finish line at Ironman Wisconsin was not the best part of the journey. There are a number of things outlined in this book that rank far higher than that. One of them is teamwork.

Going into Ironman Wisconsin, Aaron and I strategized of how we could leverage the strengths of one another to make sure that we crossed the finish line.

Here was our plan:

The Swim: Aaron took the swim as he is a better swimmer than me.

The Bike: There are a lot of hills on the Ironman Wisconsin course. Aaron is a better climber, so he took a majority of the course. I do better on the flats, so I naturally took this area. The plan was that I would aim for speed and Aaron for climbing. Without each other, we would not have been as successful.

The Run: I took a majority of the run not only because I am a more efficient runner than Aaron, but because he used a lot of his energy on the rest of the course.

Together we reached our goal of crossing the finish line. It did not matter who did what or how much work each person did. We had a goal, and we were going to reach it. If at any time one of us needed help, the other one would take over. It was incredible.

I remember being out on the bike and run course and suffering, but at least I was suffering with people I loved, doing something that I loved. Everyone else on the course that day was doing it by themselves. They had no one next to them constantly cheering them on to keep going and help them reach that finish line. I was having the time of my life with Aaron and Katie despite the pain.

Lessons:

Stop trying to be equal. It will never happen. Aaron spent more time pulling Katie that day. There is no disputing that. That being said, if I were to be more concerned about being equal rather than accomplishing our goal, we may have never accomplished our goal.

See the gifts in people, stop focusing on the negatives. If we can leverage people for their strengths, we will be far better off.

Selflessness is an amazing gift. I love the selflessness of Aaron and Katie. The race is never just about them; it is about how we can use our combined actions to reach a common goal.

Surround yourself with people that make you better. Aaron and Katie make me a better person, and I am forever thankful for that. People will either bring you down or bring you up. Remember that, not only for the friends you keep, but also for how you treat people. Every action you take helps or hurts someone.

Apply:

Identify the major people in your life. Write down the strengths or gifts that they bring to you or help you with. When you are done, create a list for yourself. Focus on how you can help others and how they can help you.

Notes: TEAMWORK

EMBRACE THE SUCK

There is a saying in Ironman that it is not a matter of if you will hurt, but rather, when you will hurt. This saying is also true in life. We are told that we should avoid pain because it is a sign of weakness. I disagree. We will all experience pain. It will either be the pain of embracing the suck or of realizing just how much we missed out on.

Training for and during Ironman there were many times when I had the choice to either embrace the suck or to avoid it. One would lead me to the finish line while the other would take me away from it.

The biggest experience of embracing the suck during Ironman would be out on the bike course. It was the hardest and longest part of course.

On the course there are three major hills that you have to climb, twice. The great thing is that for a majority of the bike these hills are crowded with people. On both sides of the road you have people cheering you on, wearing crazy costumes and blaring music to keep you going.

The first loop we did we had all the people out there, and it was incredible. It was easy to climb up those hills and to get to the top. Okay, maybe not easy, but easier than if you were all by yourself.

The second loop was a lot different. It was later in the day and close to the cutoff times. Many of the people that were cheering on the first loop had left to watch their friends and family complete the run course. Climbing these hills was a lot harder. It would have been easy for us to give up and just quit, but that is not what we wanted to do. We took on great pain to get to where we wanted to go.

Our goal in life should not be to avoid pain, but rather to embrace it. Pain is a sign of growth. It is a sign of stepping outside of your comfort zone to become an even greater version of yourself than you are today. Pain is where your growth occurs, and that is the key to life. If you are not growing, then what are you doing with your life?

Lessons:

Embracing pain is a sign of growth and becoming an even better version of yourself.

We will all experience pain. It will either be the pain of regret or the pain of embracing the suck.

To get what you really want in life, it is going to hurt, but it will be worth it.

Apply:

Take one step outside your comfort zone each day. Choose what scares you over what comforts you. There will not always be opportunities that are giant and in your face. Sometimes they will be opportunities that come to you like a ripple across a pond, but these moments will change your life.

As hard as it is, stop thinking about what can go wrong and how badly you might fail. Focus on the opportunity to grow and learn from it all. Keep a journal of all the times you have stepped outside of your comfort zone so you can see how much you kick ass.

Notes: EMBRACE THE SUCK

ABOUT THE AUTHOR

Adam Lofquist is a marketing professional that lives in Minneapolis, Minnesota. He has completed numerous marathons, ultra-marathons, triathlons and two full distance Ironman triathlons.

He most recently completed his biggest endurance athletic feat yet, a 100 mile run. He attended the University of Wisconsin – Milwaukee where he earned a degree in Marketing and Finance. He has been trained in improvisation, which makes him funny, we swear. Adam also has five years of experience in youth leadership development.

Adam helps change the mindset of the people he works with to focus on what is possible, embrace challenges and grow. He wants everyone he meets to live life to the fullest and to never be limited by their beliefs. Find out more about how Adam can help you at leadboulder.com.

Made in the USA
San Bernardino, CA
26 November 2016